DAILY
FOOTPRINT

꧁꧂

A Handbook for Today's Christian

PASTOR P.F. AJAYI

ISBN: 978-1-0370-0749-1

Published by:

MAMAX PUBLISHING.
www.maxwelloyewumi.ng/publish

For permission, write to:

Pastor Peter Friday Ajayi
114 Republic place, Randburg, Johannesburg, 2125, South

Africa.

E-mail: peterajayi17@gmail.com

This book is presented to

From

Occasion

Date

ACKNOWLEDGEMENT

I am grateful to God Almighty for the gifts of life and salvation. He is the ultimate author of this book because it is based completely on His Word.

I am also grateful to the following people: Deaconess Grace Iyabo Ajayi, my wife of more than 35 years; my blessed children, Sister Antoinette Ellis; my editor, Jesse Unoh, and my friend, publisher and fellow pastor, Maxwell Oyewumi.

INTRODUCTION

I wrote this devotional manual to mark my 60th birthday in 2020 and to accede to the demands of those who had bought and loved *Prayer That Moves Mountains*, my first book.

Regrettably, today, many Christians do not read their Bibles, and I feel they need a simple Bible reading guide such as this devotional. I hope it will be an invaluable source of help in their walk with their Creator, Jehovah.

DAY 1

FEAR NOT

Matthew 14: 24-33, 2nd Timothy 1:7

What is fear? It's a feeling you have when you are in danger. Fear is a spirit. God's word says that He has not given us a spirit of fear (2nd Timothy 1:7), and Matthew 14:27 says, "Be of good cheer; it is I; be not afraid."

Fear and faith cannot stay together.

- ◆ God is with you always – Psalm 118:6

- ◆ God is greater than your enemies – 1 John 4:4

- ◆ Do not fear people – Jeremiah 1:8

- ◆ God has promised you peace – Isaiah 26:3-11, John 16:33

Prayer point

I cast out fear and receive boldness in Jesus's name.

DAY 2

FEAR NOT (PART II)
Matthew 14:24-33, Psalm 121:1-2, Psalm 122:1-2

Jesus was walking on water and Peter asked that He command him to walk on water too. Jesus then said to Peter, "Come." It was an invitation to do what is naturally impossible.

The Bible says, "Looking unto Jesus the author and finisher of our faith..." (Hebrews 12:2) and Psalm 121:1-2 says, "I will lift up my eyes unto the hills where my help comes from?" Psalm 56:3 also declares, "The times I am afraid, I will trust in you."

Trust in the Lord. That is, depend, rely on and have confidence in God.

Causes of Fear
- Lack of faith and trust in God
- Looking at your circumstances
- Disobedience

Prayer point

I reject fear and receive faith in Jesus's name.

DAY 3

FEAR NOT (PART III)

Knowing what to do can be difficult when you're faced with certain situations. However, if you know God, go back to His promises in the Bible and apply them to your situation. Then, you can achieve clarity and success. In 2nd kings 6:15-17, Elisha prayed that God should open the eyes of his servant in a time of crisis, and God did. He saw multitudes of chariots of fire and horses.

- ◆ Trust in the Lord

- ◆ Trust in God's word (Psalm 27:1, Hebrews 13:5-6, Psalm 31:13–14, Psalm 119:165)

- ◆ Forsake sin

- ◆ Resist and rebuke the spirit of fear (Job 11:13-15)

Prayer point

Let perfect love cast out fear in Jesus's name.

DAY 4

REPENTANCE

Matthew 3:1-8

Repentance is one of the basic requirements of Christianity. It is an essential doctrine in Christianity.

What, then, is repentance? It means reviewing one's actions and feeling contrition or regret for past wrongs, with a commitment to change for the better. Repentance is a change of mind toward God, self, and sin. It is to make a U-turn.

Repentance is sincere and godly sorrow, not just remorse for being caught doing something bad. It is being sorrowful for and detesting bad actions with the true purpose of amendment. (Acts 2:38, Acts 17:30-31, Acts 3:19, 2nd Corinthians 7:10, Luke 15:10, Revelation 2:5)

Finally, repentance is a prerequisite for salvation. It is a command to all sinners and to Christians who backslide.

The blessings of repentance:

- ♦ Release from sin
- ♦ Refreshing time with God
- ♦ Forgiveness

♦ Garment of righteousness

Prayer point

I repent of all known and unknown sins in Jesus's name.

DAY 5

TRY AGAIN

Luke 5:1-11

When you have attempted any or many things in life and failed, you may be reluctant to try again. Thomas Edison tried nine hundred and ninety-nine times before he got the light bulb right at last. So, don't give up!

In the Bible, Peter was fishing and nothing was working. He thought of quitting until Jesus came and used his boat, and Peter was compensated after the period of frustration. Peter followed instructions and had a miraculous harvest; a net-breaking and boat-sinking catch.

Remember that quitters never win, and winners never quit. When God steps in, the place you failed can become a place of great success (Psalm 126, Jeremiah 32:27, Luke 1:37).

Are you frustrated in your marriage, career, Christian walk, or business? God can do more than enough. Peter saw his position of sin after the miracle. Like him, you will not catch fish anymore but will become a fisher of men. Peter forsook everything to follow Jesus.

Therefore, kingdom service is important after you have received an ultimate breakthrough.

Prayer point

I am not giving up. I will try again in Jesus's name.

DAY 6

HINDRANCES TO ANSWERED PRAYERS

James 4:2-3, Matthew 7:7, Luke 11:1-13, 1ˢᵗ Thess. 5:17, Luke 18:1-14

Prayer is the art of talking to God, worshiping Him, making our requests known to Him, thanking Him for what He has done, and praising Him for who He is.

God wants our prayers to be heard and answered. However, there are a few things that can hinder prayers. Some of these are:

1. UNFORGIVENESS

The Bible says, "Forgive us as we forgive those who have sinned against us." (Matthew 6:12, Mark 11:25. If our prayers must be answered, then we must forgive those we are holding grudges against in our hearts.

2. SIN

This refers to missing the mark and disobeying the revealed will of God. The Bible says in Psalm 66:18, "If I regard iniquity in my heart, the Lord will not hear me."

Prayer point

Let all obstacles to answered prayers give way in Jesus's name.

HINDRANCES TO ANSWERED PRAYERS (Part II)

Continuing from the hindrances to answered prayers outlined yesterday, the following are other possible hindrances.

1. WRONG MOTIVES

The Bible points out that people ask to "consume it (selfish motives) on their lust." (James 4:3 AMP) We ought to ask for things that bring glory to God and allow us to be blessings to God's creation. Although you ask God for the right things, you may not receive them because you have selfish or morally wrong motives in mind when asking.

2. PRIDE

God hates the proud. He called out Israel in 2nd Chronicles 7:14 says, "Turn from your wicked ways, humble yourself . . . I will hear from Heaven and heal your land." Also, two men went to the temple to pray; one was proud, boasting of his deeds but the publican (tax collector) prayed from afar saying, "Lord have mercy on me a sinner." He went home justified and his prayers answered.

3. FORCES OF EVIL

The devil attacks the prayers of the saints to delay their being answered. Daniel prayed and fasted for 21 days, but the prince of Persia intercepted his prayers until God sent His angels to intervene (Daniel 10:13).

Prayer point

I decree and declare that any hindrances to my answered prayer is removed in Jesus's name.

OVERCOMING TEMPTATIONS

**Matthew 4:1-11, 1ˢᵗ Corinthians 10:12-13,
Genesis 39:5-13, Proverbs 1:10, James 1:13-15**

Temptations are trials of one's faith in which one has the freedom to choose to be faithful or unfaithful to God. Temptation is an allurement or seduction to sin.

It is also the desire to do something wrong or unwise. Temptations come through what we experience through our senses such as sight and hearing. The Bible says to not consent or agree if sinners entice you (Proverbs 1:10). Joseph refused the advances of his master's wife, while Samson fell for Delilah's enticement. Jesus also overcame the temptation of the devil by using the word of God, which is the sword of the Spirit. Watch and pray to overcome sin and the works of the flesh.

- ♦ Temptation is common or universal.

- ♦ Watch out and take caution, take heed and be aware of unfriendly friends (2ⁿᵈ Corinthians 6: 14-18).

- ♦ God will always make a way of escape for you out of all temptations

- He will not permit temptation that is above what you can bear to come to you.

- Avoid places or people that can make you fall into temptation.

Prayer point

I receive power to overcome temptations in Jesus's name.

DAY 9

HOW TO OVERCOME YOUR WEAKNESSES

What is weakness?

To be weak is to lack physical strength and energy. Weakness is being liable to break or give way under pressure, or to be neither stable nor firm. Peter denied Jesus when a little girl identified him as one of his disciples. Judas Iscariot sold out his master, Jesus, to the religious leaders because of money. Samson also told Delilah the secret of his spiritual strength (Judges 16).

YOU CAN OVERCOME YOUR WEAKNESS THROUGH THE FOLLOWING WAYS

- ◆ Face your weaknesses as a sin.
- ◆ Give the Holy Spirit room to help you walk in the spirit.
- ◆ Ask your Heavenly father to take away your bad habits.
- ◆ Believe that God has given you victory over sin.
- ◆ Abide in Christ (John 15).

- ♦ Pray daily.

- ♦ Overcome temptations through prayer and fasting.

- ♦ Avoid the wrong company.

- ♦ Read the word of God regularly.

- ♦ Stay busy serving God (John 12:26, Colossians 3:23 - 24).

Prayer point

Lord, give me strength to overcome weaknesses in Jesus's name.

DAY 10

DON'T GIVE UP
Luke 5:1-11

The story in the Scripture above is about Simon Peter's encounter with Jesus Christ. Peter had a night of fishing expenditure without any results. Then Jesus showed up and asked for Peter's boat to use as a platform to preach or teach His audience. After using the boat, Jesus asked Peter to launch into the deep again. Jesus meant for Peter to stop fishing in shallow waters. Peter replied, "I have tried all I know how to but I am met with frustration." But I love Jesus's resolve for Peter to try again and when he did, he had a net-breaking and boat-sinking catch. Peter even had to beckon on his friends to help him draw the net.

Are you frustrated?

Consider the following points from the story and apply them to your situation.

- God displayed His power.
- Peter allowed Jesus to use his boat. So, value God's word.

- Jesus told Peter what to do (divine direction).

- Peter saw how sinful he was and that only God can forgive.

- Discover your assignment. Peter became a fisher of men.

- Peter left everything and followed Jesus (Proverbs 3:5-6, Psalm 32: 8-9, Jeremiah 32:27).

Prayer point

I refuse to give up. My problems will be the ones to give up.

DAY 11

DON'T GIVE UP (Part II)
John 5

Jesus met a man at the pool of Bethesda, which means the house of mercy, who had been there for 38 years. He was waiting for almost forever for the moving of the water.

An angel normally came to stir the water and the man watched the people get healed before his eyes. Then Jesus asked if he wanted to be made whole? Instead of answering, "Yes," he said, "I have no man." I pray for you, may God send you a man or a woman to push you into your next level in Jesus's name.

Jesus saw the man in and out and He knew how long he had been in that case. So He said, "Rise up, take your bed and go home." Your case may not be as bad as this man with no name, but Jesus is saying to you today to rise up above your sickness, career, challenges, marriage conflicts, failure in business and make progress, succeed and prosper. Will you rise today and be all that God created you to be because the time is now? Leave your excuses and discouragements and make a move. God is ahead of you; don't give up.

My problems, give up now in Jesus's name.

DAY 12

◦◦◦❦◦◦◦

BARTIMAEUS, THE BLIND MAN

Mark 10:46-52

As Jesus and His disciples were leaving Jericho, a multitude of people were also leaving the city. Bartimaeus, a blind man, could hear the people's footsteps and he asked, "What is going on?" They replied that Jesus of Nazareth was passing through where he regularly begged. I pray that God deliver you from the spirit of begging and poverty in Jesus' name.

Bartimaeus had a problem: lack of sight or blindness. He was stagnant, blind to people and opportunities around him. His destiny and time were wasting. I pray that God will restore all your wasted years in Jesus's name. So, Bartimaeus cried aloud saying, "Jesus, son of David, Have mercy on me!" Don't keep quiet, cry to God for mercy for He is abundant in mercy.

The crowd tried to shut him up. They told him to keep quiet but he cried out the more, and eventually got the attention of Jesus. Interestingly, the same crowd that had tried to shut him up told him, "Jesus is calling you." My friend, Jesus is calling you today.

Then Jesus asked him, "What do you want me to do for you?" He replied, "That I may regain my sight." I command that you regain your sight of opportunities, marriage, business potential, and progress in Jesus's name.

Jesus told blind Bartimaeus, "Your faith has made you whole," and he was he was healed immediately (Mark 10:52). Have faith in God. Hebrews 11:6 says without faith it is impossible to please God. Jesus Christ is the anchor of our faith and He is the same yesterday, today, and forever (Hebrews 13:8).

Prayer point

In the name of Jesus, my faith makes me whole.

DAY 13

RESIST THE DEVIL AND HE WILL FLEE

James 4:7-10

1. Submit yourselves therefore to God. Resist the devil and he will flee from you.

2. Draw near to God and he will draw near to you.

3. Cleanse your hands you sinners, and purify your hearts, you double-minded.

4. Be afflicted and mourn and weep. Let your laughter be turned to mourning and joy to heaviness.

5. Humble yourselves in the sight of the Lord and He shall lift you up.

To resist is to refuse to accept something. It means trying to stop something from happening. I pray you refuse to accept the sickness, death, attacks, sorrows, failures, disappointment, depression and fear in the name of Jesus. Try to stop all that the witches and forces of darkness has planted for you like accidents and all forms of losses from happening in Jesus's name.

Your question might be, "How do I oppose, resist, stop things from happening, and refuse to accept what the devil is offering?"

- ♦ By ceaselessly praying. Don't wait for trouble before you pray (1ˢᵗ Thessalonians 5:17). Also, Luke 18:1 says, "Men ought to pray without giving up."

- ♦ Know the promises of God and stand upon them in the time of temptation and trial. In Matthew 4:1–11, Jesus responded to all the devils' temptations with, "It is written..."

- ♦ Be steadfast. It means to be firm in what you believe. Don't easily give up (Galatians 5:1, 1ˢᵗ Corinthians 16:13).

- ♦ Acts 16:25-26 when you pray, God sends angels, but when you praise Him, He comes by Himself.

Prayer point

In Jesus name, I resist the devil.

DAY 14

LOVE

1 Corinthians 13:1-14, John 3:16, Romans 5:5-8

This is a central topic in the Christian faith.

What is love? Love is aggressive, goodwill and sacrificial kindness. And God's love remains the eternal and universal standard. "For God so loved the world that He gave His only begotten son . . ." (John 3:16).

Love is God and God is love. Love is an attitude we have to learn. It is universal. Jesus said that when we love one another then shall men know that we are His disciples (Hebrews 13:1). Let brotherly love continue.

Love freely, honestly without deceit and unconditionally. The love we are talking about is agape; the God kind of love.

Characteristics of love

- ◆ Love is patient
- ◆ Love is kind
- ◆ Love is not rude
- ◆ Love is not selfish

- Love believes in all things no matter the problem
- Love bears all things and has hope

Don't hate or kill yourself. God loves you. Receive God's love and go out of your way to help strangers. Many are looking for love in the wrong places.

Everything will end but hope, faith and love abide forever. Love the Lord with all your heart, soul and spirit. Love your neighbour as yourself.

Prayer point

May the love of God fill my heart in Jesus's name.

DAY 15

CURSES

Galatians 3:13-14, Proverbs 26:2

Curses are negative pronouncements spoken or unspoken on people or self-imposed. Curses are an empowerment to fail.

Prayer point

I break the curses of sin, sickness and poverty in my life in Jesus's name.

HAVE FAITH IN GOD

Mark 11:22-25, Hebrews 11:1-6

Hebrew 11:1 says that faith is the substance of things hoped for, the evidence of things not seen. It is the connecting power into the spiritual realm which links us to God and makes Him become tangible to a person's sense perception. In Greek, PISTIS means to believe; to rely on what a person says or to act on their word. Belief, persuasion, assurance, firm conviction and faithfulness, confidence in hope (expectation), assurance that God is working even though we cannot see it; these are all the meanings of faith. See Romans 4:16-21 and Mark 11:22-24. It is impossible to please God without faith. He who comes to God must believe and that He is the rewarder of those who seek Him diligently.

Prayer point

I put my faith in God's word in Jesus's name.

DAY 17

GODLINESS AND CONTENTMENT IS GREAT GAIN

1st Timothy 6:10

What is godliness? It is reverence for God, fear of God, awe, respect, honour for God, and obedience to God's law. It is the reverential fear of God. It is to be consecrated to God, set apart, or dedicated or devoted to God.

Contentment means satisfaction, happiness and being pleased with what you have achieved in line with your expectation. There is gain in living to please God. The Bible says we came without nothing to this world and when we go back to God, we will not go with anything.

Many people are doing things to get gain: making people to cry, cheating, prostitution, ritual killings and so on. We don't need much to be contented; we just need to be grateful for everything we have: love, good health, work, family and such things are what we cannot buy with money.

Gain means profit from godliness and satisfaction. Those who want to become rich overnight fall into hurtful and foolish temptations, and destruction and perdition. The Bible encourages us not to trust in uncertain riches but to trust in the living God (Proverbs 3:5-6).

Prayer point

Father, help me to be godly and content.

THE BLESSING OF THE LORD

Proverbs 10:22, Genesis 1:22, 28, Deuteronomy 28:1-14, Malachi 3:8-12

What is a blessing? It is an empowerment to succeed, to stay protected and favoured. To bring to pass what you have been expecting and having God's support and approval is what blessing means. God adds to you to be prosperous, accomplished and to make it in life (Psalm 1:2-3).

So, what can you do to key into God's blessing?

- ◆ Obey God and follow His instructions.
- ◆ Remember God (Deuteronomy 8:18).
- ◆ Give tithes and offerings.
- ◆ Meditate on God's word.
- ◆ Engage in sacrificial giving.
- ◆ Have integrity.
- ◆ Work hard.

Purpose of God's blessing

Genesis 12:1-3 talks about how Abraham is God's blessing.

- ◆ To meet your needs.
- ◆ To help the poor.
- ◆ To support God's kingdom.

(Galatians 3:13-14, Joshua 1:8)

Prayer point

Oh Lord, bless me and make me a blessing.

DAY 19

HONOUR

Proverbs 3:9-10, 1ˢᵗ Samuel 2:30, Ephesians 6:2

Honour your father and your mother is the first commandment with a promise. God also says that He will honor whoever honours Him and those who despise Him, He will lightly esteem.

What does it mean to honour a person or a thing? It means to give weight, add value, or respect. We must honor God for who He is and what He is doing. God must be a priority in our lives because He deserves it. Also, we should honour our fathers and mothers. This is a commandment that attracts long life and prosperity. It is Biblical to honour pastors, prophets or spiritual leaders, and political leaders too. Husbands, honour your wives; wives, honour your husbands. We must maintain the culture of honour (Matthew 10: 40-42).

Prayer point

Lord, help me to honour you in all I do.

DAY 20

THE PROMISES OF GOD
Psalm 91:10-11, Hebrews 13:2, Psalm 34:7

What is a promise? It is an assurance that one will do something or that something will happen. In the Bible, thousands of the promises God made took place after many years. Abraham was promised a child (Isaac) that only came to pass after twenty-five years. In Genesis 21:1-3, Isaac was born. In 2nd Kings 7, the Prophet Elisha promised that food would be surplus and it happened in twenty-four hours.

God promised that a saviour would be born to save the whole world (Isaiah 9:6, Isaiah 7:14 Matthew 1:21, 23). And the promise was fulfilled hundreds of years later. Numbers 23:19 says that God is not a man to lie nor a son of man to repent; when He says a thing, He fulfils it. Every promise in the word of God is mine because I am standing on the promise that cannot fail. This should be your attitude too.

Prayer point

Father, I stand on your promises.

DAY 21

BREAKING LIMITATIONS

2nd Kings 4:1-7, John 1:46, Jeremiah 32:27

A limit is a point, line, or level beyond which something does not, or may not exceed.

So many people are limiting themselves but God wants you to go far in your business, ministry, and all aspects of life. Your level of faith may be holding you back to a spot. Many have allowed negative voices from inside, or their friends and family to talk them down. Do not let your handicap hold you back or to a spot.

Confess the following. I am who God says I am, I can do what God says I can do, and I can reach where God says I can reach in my business, academics, career, and life etc.

Examples of Bible characters who broke limitations are:

- ♦ The woman with the issue of blood
- ♦ Jabez
- ♦ Jephthah

Is there anything too hard for God? Have faith in God and remove limitations from your mind.

Prayer point

Oh Lord, grant me the strength to break all my limitations.

DAY 22

ANGELS OF GOD

Psalm 91:10-11, Hebrews 13:2, Psalm 34:7, Hebrews 1:14, 2nd Kings 6:17

Angels are God's bodyguards. They are God's messengers sent to different people in the Bible both in the old and new testaments. Angels appeared to Jacob, Gideon, Daniel and Isaiah.

Angels are of different classes:

- Those who deliver messages from God such as Angel Gabriel

- Those who fight for God's people such as Angel Michael

Angels were there at Jesus's birth. After His temptation, angels ministered to Him. At the garden of Gethsemane, angels also strengthened Jesus. Also at His death and resurrection, angels played a prominent role.

Billy Graham wrote a book titled *Angels, God's Secret Agents*. That is precisely who they are. In our world today, angels have appeared to persons in danger and they were miraculously delivered and protected while on assignment for the master, God. Angels are mighty and many. In Psalms 91, God promised angelic protection and visitation like in the case of Manoah, the father of Gideon, who was one of the Judges of Israel.

Prayer point

I release your angels to protect and deliver me in Jesus's name.

DAY 23

DIVINE HELP

Psalm 121, Psalm 124:8, Hebrews 4:16, Isaiah 41:10-14

To help is to make things easier and better; to give something to those who need it. It equally means to aid, support, or assist. Psalm 121:2 says, "I will look unto the hill from where comes my help?" Help means to satisfy a need and to contribute strength or to cooperate effectively.

As Christians, our help comes from above and not from abroad. Help is a necessity in life. The rich need help just like the poor; the old and young also need help. We all need one form of help or the other. Help could be spiritual, material, financial, or in other forms. God can help and He is ever willing to help us. He is a loving God and can put people on our paths to help us where and when we need them.

In Isaiah 41:10-14, the words, "I will help you" appear three times. Rely on God, look up to Him and seek Him. What you make happen for people God will also make happen for you. The Bible says, "Come boldly to the throne to obtain mercy to help in time of need." (Hebrews 4:16). May God place destiny helpers on your path to destiny in the name of Jesus.

Prayer point

I receive help from above and also human help.

DAY 24

COMMITMENT
Luke 9:57-62

Commitment is to be loyal, and faithful to a person or a thing. In our context, it is wholly following the Lord. Most people want change but do not want to change. If you are going to be a leader, then "commitment" must be a familiar word in your vocabulary. Commitment is a promise. The Bible wants us to serve God without looking back. We should be willing to work and give energy to God's cause of God (Psalm 22:8, Matthew 19:27-29, 2nd Chronicles 16:9, Luke 9:23, Mark 10:42-45, Hosea 9:4).

Commitment also includes making a decision openly. Jesus said we should confess Him openly and not be ashamed of Him (Romans 1:16). Be committed to prayer, Bible study, going to church, preaching the Gospel to the unbelievers, and living a transparent life. When we are committed to our career, marriage, or something else, it means that we stand for something. You either stand for something or fall for anything. So, faithfully adhere to your beliefs. We should also reject instant gratification and vote for delayed gratification as we shun the alluring traps of vices.

Furthermore, your commitment will be tested in issues concerning money and time, and how you spend them. Commitment brings about accomplishment of the task. If you want to give room for higher goals as students, workers and apprentices, then commitment is a must.

Prayer point

The grace to be committed to God and my assignment, I receive in Jesus's name.

DAY 25

OBSTACLES TO SALVATION
Luke 19:1-10 (King James Version)

Verses 1–5 says, "And Jesus entered and passed through Jericho. And behold, there was a man named Zacchaeus, which was the chief among the publicans, and he was rich. And he sought to see Jesus who he was; and could not for the press, because he was little of stature. And he ran before and climbed up into a sycamore tree to see him: for he was to pass that way. And when Jesus came to the place, he looked up, and saw him, and said unto him, Zacchaeus, make haste, and come down; for today I must abide at thy house."

When Jesus entered and passed through Jericho, an important and prosperous city, Zacchaeus risked ridicule to see Jesus by climbing the sycamore tree. He genuinely wanted to see Jesus. The Bible records that he could not see Jesus because of his small stature. We have to remove hindrances and obstacles. Jesus told him, "I am the way, the truth, and the life." Don't climb through means like religion, rituals, or the traditions of men. It is a relationship with God that counts, not religion.

Remove pride and arrogance. Zacchaeus was a short man and acknowledged this. All have sinned and come short of God's glory. His natural state gave him a disadvantage. The crowd hindered Zacchaeus's meeting or seeing Jesus. Jesus came to Jairus's house and put the crowd out. He went into the house with Peter, John, and James, and Jairus's daughter was healed. You need to keep the crowd (fear, doubt, and discouragement) out to allow faith and God's miracle-working power into your life and situation. God is willing to serve you. Jesus is inviting Himself into your house. Humble yourself and let Him in. Do not allow Him to keep standing outside knocking at the door (Revelation 3:20, Acts 4:12, Romans 10:9-10, John 1:12).

Prayer point

I dismantle every obstacle to salvation and deliverance in Jesus's name.

DAY 26

❦

GRATITUDE

1ˢᵗ Thessalonians 5:18, Luke 17:11-17

Give thanks in all things. When last did you say, "Thank you, Jesus?"

Be thankful for your life. We live in a world where people are ungrateful. This is apart from other words like please or sorry, which are in short supply today. The Bible says that in the last days, people shall be unthankful and unholy. Jesus showed the importance of gratitude in the following instances.

♦ Bringing Lazarus back to life (John 11:41-43). This shows that when you praise God dead situations come back to life.

♦ The ten lepers were healed, but only one came back to testify. Jesus said, "Be made whole," and his healing was perfected (Ephesians 5:20, Acts 16:25, Philippians 4:6, Psalms 103:1-2). Also, the five loaves and two fish were multiplied for Jesus to share to the five thousand. May your joy, health, business, and blessings multiply as you praise and thank God. The

Bible says to give thanks to God for He is good, and His mercy endures forever. May God do a notable thing in your life that will make you organise thanksgiving in your church in Jesus's name.

Prayer point

In Jesus's name, I reject the spirit of murmuring and I claim the garment of praise.

DAY 27

DIVINE PROVISION

Genesis 22:1-14, Philippians 4:19

This means using God's power to meet human needs (2nd Peter 1:3, Job 38:41, John 10:10, Luke 12:7, 24, Philippians 4:6, Psalm 23:1, Psalm 37:25). God created man, and He desires to meet every need that man has or could ever have. He proved this by taking time to create everything man will ever need, and then made man the crown of His creation.

God created Adam and provided him with Eve to take care of his need for companionship. Thousands of years later, God asked Abraham to sacrifice his son to test his faith. Abraham showed willingness to obey God's command and then God provided a ram for the sacrifice. Elijah still enjoyed a steady provision of food and water even after the brook had dried up. When there is a need, it may mean you are not in the right location (1st Kings 17:1-16). May God give you divine direction to where your needs will be met miraculously.

Apart from divine direction, obedience to the voice of God is vital if you are to enjoy uncommon supply. Ephesians 3:20

says that God can give you far beyond what you can think or ask. He will supply, by Christ Jesus, the riches of His glory. He became poor so that through His poverty you might be rich. He is our shepherd and we will not lack (Psalm 23:1).

I was young now I am old; I have never seen the righteous forsaken or their seed begging bread (Psalm 37:25). I have ceaseless supply from God since I became a Christian. May God provide all your needs in Jesus's name. He makes a way even in the wilderness and provides water in the desert.

Prayer point

Father, supply my needs according to your riches in glory.

DAY 28

WALKING WITH GOD

Genesis 17:1-2, Genesis 3:8, Ephesians 5:2,8,
2ⁿᵈ Corinthians 5:7, Amos 3:3, Genesis 6:9

What does it mean to walk with God? It means to be on the same page with God. To be in tune with Him, to be current and in step with God. To walk with God is to have constant and regular fellowship with Him, which entails having a personal and close relationship with him.

Our predecessors in the Bible have this testimony that they walked with God, sought Him, pleased, and obeyed Him promptly. Fellowship has to do with sharing. You share your joys, sorrows, challenges, and fears with God through prayer and fasting. Jesus woke up early in the morning to seek God's face (His presence) to draw strength from His source (Psalm 42:1, Psalm 16:11).

God has called us to be His friend just like Abraham was His friend. God wants us to walk in love and light. The Bible says that whoever walks in the light will see clearly and shall not stumble in darkness or be overpowered by darkness. Jesus is the light of the world. He wants us to walk in the spirit not to be controlled by the works of the flesh. God told Abraham, "Walk before me and be perfect."

Micah 6:8 says, "He has shown you, O man, what is good; and what does the Lord require of you. But to do justly, to love mercy, and to walk humbly with your God? Psalm 1:1 says, "Blessed is the man who walks not in the counsel of the ungodly, nor stands in the path of sinners, nor sits in the seat of the scornful."

Prayer point

Abraham and Enoch walked closely with you, Lord. Let my relationship also be intimate with you.

DAY 29

LOSE HIM AND LET HIM GO

John 11:1-44

Jesus is everything He said He is. He is the light of the world, the good shepherd, and the way, the truth and the life. In Job 19:25 Job said, "I know that my redeemer lives."

Jesus equally said, "I am the resurrection and the life (John 11:25-26). In this long passage of John 11, we read about Mary, Martha, and their brother Lazarus. The message highlighted the following:

- Lazarus
- He who you love is sick
- This sickness is not unto death but that the son of God may be glorified
- Jesus stayed two days more
- Lord if you were here he wouldn't have died
- The master has come
- Roll away the stone
- By this time he is stinking

- If you believe, you will see the glory of God
- Thank you that you hear me always
- Lazarus come forth
- Lose him and let him go

Lazarus, whose name means he who God loves, and his family were loved by Jesus. God loves all and you can enjoy God's love. God loves you (Jeremiah 31:3, Romans 5:8), but it does not exempt us from the challenges of life. That problem or challenge you face will not kill you, instead, you will come out better. So, don't give up or be bitter because your dry bones shall live again to the glory of God (Romans 8:28).

Also, know that delay is not denial. Jesus stayed back two extra days. People could see that Lazarus did not go into a coma but was actually confirmed dead and had been buried for four days. What you must know is that God never comes too early or too late. He always comes at the right time (Jeremiah 1:12, Psalm 70).

Lazarus's sisters exclaimed, '

"Lord, if you were here, Lazarus would not have died." Jesus makes a difference in people's lives. Give him a chance to show up in your life and situation. Let Jesus come in.

Hebrew 13:8 says that Jesus is the same yesterday, today, and forever. Malachi 3:6 says, "I am the Lord, I change not, the children of Jacob are not consumed." The Master arrived and the story changed. As a songwriter wrote, "*If you are tired of the load of your sin, let Jesus come into your heart. Just now, your doubting disown. Just now, reject Him no more.*"

Jesus said, "Roll away the stone," but Lazarus's family said, "By now, it is too late. Lazarus should be stinking. It is a hopeless situation." And Jesus replied, "If you believe, you will see the glory of God." Then He shouted, "Lazarus, come forth!" Roll away the stone of doubt and fear in your life and come out of the cave of discouragement and failure. Lazarus came out with his hands and feet tied. May your feet be loosened so you can walk again, gain mobility, and move forward. May your hands be loosened to grip good things in your life.

When Jesus finished His job, He told Lazarus's sisters and bystanders, "Loosen him and let him go." You are loosened from the ancient chains of your father and mother in Jesus's name. Jesus delayed in going to Bethany, where Lazarus lived, which was just two miles (a little over two kilometres) from Jerusalem. Many people would want to know why He did that to His friend. It was because He wanted to use Lazarus to tell the world that no matter how a situation has degenerated, it could still be reversed if only He is brought into the picture.

Prayer point

Lord, loose me and let me go.

DAY 30

DIVINE WISDOM

1st Kings 3: 1-13, Proverbs 1:7, Proverbs 4:7, James 1:5, James 3:13–18

Wisdom is the ability to use your knowledge and experience to make decisions. It is the application of knowledge. It is also the ability to discern between good and evil, and to make sensible decisions. In Proverbs 1:7, the Bible says, "The fear of God is the beginning of knowledge, but fools despise wisdom and instruction." Proverbs 4:7 declares, "Wisdom is the principal thing and with all thy getting, get understanding."

James 3:13-18 tells us of the different kinds of wisdom that exist.

1. Sensual wisdom (commonsense)
2. Earthly wisdom
3. Devilish wisdom
4. Wisdom from above.

Sensual or natural wisdom is day-to-day wisdom. Earthly wisdom is the wisdom from secular books and human philosophy. Devilish wisdom is the wisdom from the devil, which is full of cunning, and crafty ideas. Divine wisdom is the wisdom that is from above and divine; it also comes with meekness.

Someone once said, "Meekness is not weakness but power in disguise." This kind of wisdom is not with strife and does not tell lies against the truth. Wisdom from above is rather characterised by purity. It is not contaminated, but peaceful, sensual, easy to be entreated, full of mercy and has the fruits of righteousness, rightly positioned right living. Wisdom from above has no partiality and hypocrisy (pretending to be what you are not).

How do You get Wisdom?

- James 1:5 says, "If any of you lacks wisdom, let him ask God that giveth to all men liberally and upbraided not: and it shall be given him." This is the way to get wisdom. Asking God like Solomon did in 1ˢᵗ Kings 3. When Solomon asked God for wisdom, He gave him a blank cheque.

- Through our life's experiences.

♦ We can acquire wisdom from books written by men and women through their wealth of experience.

You and I need wisdom to grow in life, so build a healthy marriage relationship, business, career, and other aspects of your life. Jesus is the wisdom of God.

- "Knowledge is knowing what to say, wisdom is knowing when to say it." –Anonymous.
- "The invariable mark of wisdom is to see the miraculous in the common." –Ralph Waldo Emerson.
- "Knowledge is learning something every day. Wisdom is letting go of something every day." –Zen Proverb.
- "Honesty is the first book of wisdom." –Thomas Jefferson.
- "Wisdom is knowing the right path to take, integrity is taking it." –Anonymous.
- "Wisdom is the right use of knowledge" –Charles Spurgeon.

Prayer point

Help me to fear you, oh Lord. For that is beginning of wisdom.

DAY 31

❦

ELIJAH, AN ORDINARY MAN
1ˢᵗ Kings 18:1-46, James 5:17-18

Prophet Elijah was an ordinary man who was used in an extraordinary way in times of crises. Among the characters in the Bible, especially in the old testament, two people stand out for me. The first is Joseph in matters of character and integrity. The second is Elijah, a man of power and prayer. He was a man who locked up Heaven and put the key in his pocket. He was the prophet who called down fire and opened Heaven for mighty rain. Elijah showed up in the time of apostasy, crises, famine, discouragement, fear, and despair. He was a man of faith and prayer.

Prayer point

Lord, use me like you used Elijah in Jesus's name.

DAY 32

WHAT TO DO IN TIMES OF TROUBLE

**Psalm 46:1-10, Psalm 50:15,
Jeremiah 33:3, Job 14:1, Job 5:19-24**

Job said that troublesome times are always going to come. Proverbs 24:10 says that if you faint in the time of adversity, it means your strength is small. People fear and get into depression over the issues of life. But there are a few things you can do in times of trouble or crises.

- Pray in the time of trouble and God will give you an idea of what to do. God said when you call, He will show you great and mighty things.

- We need to confess and forsake our sins (Isaiah 59:1-2). Psalm 66:18 says, "If I regard iniquity in my heart, the Lord will not hear me." (Proverbs 28:18)

- Seek God's face, pray the prayer of enquiries. Ask God for your next line of action. David enquired from God. He was told to pursue, overtake, and recover all from the enemies of his people (1st Samuel 30:16–19).

- In times of trouble, we are to trust in the Lord and acknowledge Him in all our ways (Proverbs 3:5-6, Isaiah 26:3-4).

- Confess your sins to God and turn from your wicked ways (Psalm 51, 1st John 1:7-9). 2nd Chronicles 7:14 says, "If my people who are called by name shall turn from their wicked ways and humble themselves and pray, I will hear from Heaven and heal their land."

- In times of crisis or trouble, it is good to give, make sacrificial sowing of seeds, and pay your tithes (Genesis 26).

- Psalm 126:5-6 says, "Those who sow in tears shall reap in joy. Those who sow their precious seeds shall come back rejoicing."

- Give thanks in times of trouble or crises. 1st Thessalonians 5:18 says, "In all things give thanks. For this is the will of God for you in Christ Jesus." What you have multiplies when you give thanks and praise God. Dead situations also come to life.

Prayer point

In the time of trouble I choose to trust You, Lord, in Jesus's name.

DAY 33

THE GRACE OF GOD

Romans 6:1-2, Ephesians 2: 8–9, 1st Corinthians 15:10, 2nd Corinthians 9:8

Grace is unmerited kindness and favour from God. It is God's desire that we grow in His grace (2nd Peter 3:18).

We were sinners who did not qualify for God's grace, but God sent Jesus to give His life for us so that we can enjoy His favour.

Prayer point

May I know that your grace is sufficient for me in Jesus's name.

DAY 34

SPIRITUAL GROWTH

2ⁿᵈ Peter 3:16, Hebrews 5:12–14, 1ˢᵗ Peter 2:2, 1ˢᵗ
Corinthians 13:11,
1ˢᵗ Corinthians 3:1–4, 1ˢᵗ Peter 3:18

What is growth? Growth is to advance, develop, and increase in size and stature. It is to gain full age, maturity, and the ability to discern between good and evil. It is also to put off childish behaviour. Growth is and should be the goal of every Christian. The Bible shows us the signs of not growing, which include strife, bitterness, being easily provoked, gossiping, backbiting, not being stable with the things of God, not forgiving easily, etc. Those who are not growing always complain about how no one is following them up, yet they lack time for prayer, regular fasting, and fellowship with God.

In 1ˢᵗ Corinthians 13:11, Paul talked about the way to speak. There is how babies speak and there is how adults speak. Also, the understanding: you must strive to understand God and people. You also need to understand the principles of life and you need foresight, insight, and hindsight to do this. To grow physically, you need to check your diet, discipline, exercise, etc. Just as you eat right; a proper diet that has nutrients for your growth, you need the word of God as spiritual food to energise and give you stamina for the race of life (1ˢᵗ Peter 2:2).

Just like you need air to breathe, you also need the Holy Spirit (Ephesians 5:18, Acts 1: 8). To grow spiritually you need regular devotion to cultivate a personal relationship with God in prayer. You need to hear God regularly, and you also need to fellowship with other believers in regular attendance of church services like Bible study, prayer meetings, seminars, house fellowships and other programmes stipulated by the church and ministry (Hebrews 10:25).

The more you serve God using your abilities, talents and gifts, the more you grow.

Prayer point

Lord, help me to grow in my spiritual life.

DAY 35

❦

TITHE AND OFFERING

Malachi 3:8-12, Leviticus 27:30

Tithe is ten percent of your income. Offering is anything that you give beyond that. The issue of tithe has generated controversy, but let the Bible speak for itself. My take is that God wants us to give tithes and pay our offerings.

Prayer point

May I be faithful in tithes and offerings in Jesus's name.

DAY 36

IDOL WORSHIP

Exodus 20:4

An idol is an image or representation of a god used as an object of worship. It is also a thing or person greatly admired, loved or revered. Whatever you place high value on is your God. In times past, most of our fathers served trees, wood, stones, rivers, carved images and so on. Today, idols are no longer carved images but fancy things, computers, cell phones, careers, sex, beauty, celebrities, and music to name but a few. The Bible warns against false gods, statues, images, and anything you love more than God. Don't make for yourself idols. They are not worthy of worship or praise.

God is a jealous God. Do not transfer His worship and honour to a rival. Idolatry brings physical brokenness, pain, suffering, and death. An idolatrous heart craves for the things God hates.

Consequences of idol worship.

- It brings God down from the throne of our hearts by not making Him first place in our lives (Exodus 20:1-6, Exodus 34:14, 17, Hosea 2:15, Hosea 4:12).

- It is rebellion.

- It is a sign that we hate God.

- It belittles God (1st Corinthians 10:14, 19-22, Deuteronomy 6:5-6).

- Idols occupy the space meant for God –Martin Lloyd-Jones

Anything that has a controlling position, what you depend on and takes too much of your time, attention, energy and money arouses God's displeasure. It brings destruction. Remember God and thank Hi, for sending Jesus to save the world.

Prayer point

May I focus my heart on Your word so I can succeed in Jesus's name.

DAY 37

KEYS TO SUCCESS

Joshua 1:8

Success means to accomplish a long-time dream. The Longman Dictionary of Contemporary English defines success as achieving of something you have been trying to do. It is something that has a good result or effect, or someone who does very well in their job. It also means to be happy with what you have. You should not be an NFA (no future ambition). Success is a journey.

Dennis Kimbro in his book, *What Makes the Great, Great* says, "You cannot succeed being like everybody else. You must take that lonely road." The journey into your mind. Your greatest asset is righteousness, and the best advice is for you to work hard. The biggest secret is that you are already rich, and the greatest victory is the triumph of human spirit. Your greatest need is prayer and the greatest story ever told about you is that of leaving a legacy.

Prayer point

May I apply the keys to success in Jesus's name.

DAY 38

KEYS TO SUCCESS (PART II)
Joshua 1:8, Psalm 1

In part 1, we defined the meaning of the word success as a journey. There are keys to success, and we will take them one after the other.

In Joshua 1:8, the key words are "This law shall not depart from your mouth." To meditate means to ponder, to think over something for a long time. Chew it over before you swallow it, pay attention, observe, and get the message in the letter, the spiritual import, and deeper meaning in the words and sentences. So, to succeed in life, the word of God is key number one.

Secondly, to succeed in life, there is the need to live right. Righteous living or being rightly positioned with God is a prerequisite. Matthew 6: 33 says, "Seek ye first the kingdom of God and its righteousness and all these things shall be added unto you." Do your business, marriage, and ministry God's way. Then success will be achievable (Proverbs 14:34).

Thirdly, your association is very important. The friends you keep will tell me where you are going in life. Your association is like an escalator that either takes you up or down in life. Show me your friends, they say, and I will tell you who you are. You cannot say you want to quit stealing when your friends are thieves. Proverbs 1:10 says, "My son, if sinners entice thee, consent thou not." 1st Corinthians 15:33 says, "Evil communication corrupts good manners." Integrity is a key factor in the matter of success. Live above board. A life without integrity is a cheap life. People watch the life you live secretly and publicly. It should not be a case of public success and private failure. People want to be sure that you can be trusted before they can have dealings with you. Integrity determines how you deal with money, the opposite sex, secrets, and moral issues.

May you follow the principles for success in every sphere of your life in Jesus' name.

Prayer point

Help me to set achievable goals, forget about yesterday, be diligent and win in life.

DAY 39

KEYS TO SUCCESS (PART III)

There are so many keys to success

- Determination
- Prayer
- Forgetting yesterday's failure
- Set achievable goals
- Value time
- Try something new
- Persistence
- Believe in God
- Planning
- Information
- Diligence
- Enthusiasm
- Sacrifice
- Courage

Determination: Is firmness of purpose. It is the process of establishing something exactly by calculating or researching. Another word that explains determination is the focus you need to get something done. School projects, building projects, ministry, Christian walk, relationships, careers, and so on require determination.

It enables us to persist in the face of difficulties. Daniel 1:8 says, "But Daniel purposed in his heart that he would not defile himself with the portion of the king's delicacies, nor with the wine which he drank; therefore, he requested of the chief of the eunuchs that he might not defile himself. Now God had brought Daniel into the favour and goodwill of the chief of the eunuchs."

God brought Daniel into favour and tender love with the prince of the eunuchs. It is better to die for something than to live for nothing. At the early stage of our Christian journey, we might sin. But, as we mature our daily song should be, *"I have decided to follow Jesus, no turning back. I have got my mind made up that won't go back."* The journey into success and significance is full of fear, discouragement, and disappointments. It requires a resolve to stay focused. Hebrews 12:2 says, "Looking unto Jesus the author and finisher of our faith."

Prayer: Is the key to success. It is a dynamic tool that the world has yet to fully exploit. Prayer is key to victory over the forces of evil that can deter any man on the path of progress and success. Prayer is making our worship and request to God. "Life is fragile, handle with prayer" -Bumper sticker

"Key to power to transform your life. Passport to success, your visa to happiness and wellbeing, your hidden guide to human progress." –Dennis Kimbro, *What Makes the Great, Great.* See Matthew 7:7-11, Philippians 4:6-7, Jeremiah 33:3, James 5:16-18.

Goal-setting: Is to a man what a compass is to a ship. It is the map that leads the road. You must have goals for the things you want to achieve and those goals should be easy for you to understand, they should be long-term and short-term goals. In life, the following are important in helping you achieve your goals.

- ♦ Information
- ♦ Diligence
- ♦ Sacrifice
- ♦ Courage

Prayer point

Father, give me the grace to do all I need to be a success in Jesus's name.

MAN'S EXTREMITY IS THE BEGINNING OF GOD'S MIRACLE

Matthew 9:18-26, Mark 5:28-43, Jeremiah 32:27, Luke 1:37,45, Malachi 3:6

Extremity is the farthest point or limit of a thing. A miracle is something that happens beyond nature. It is an extraordinary and welcome event believed to be the work of God. The Bible is the Bible because of the miracles recorded from Genesis to Revelation. We are talking of the extraordinary occurrences performed in the lives of people who took the steps of faith and the miracles performed as a sign to authenticate the truth that God is alive.

When man has come to an end of what he can do all by himself, then God takes over. Man's extremity is an open door for God to prove himself. Jairus, the ruler of the synagogue, heard about Jesus's miracles, teachings, and claims. He was humble, and loved his daughter. He also believed Jesus could heal her. What do you think was in his mind when he heard that his daughter had finally died? He was heartbroken. But God is the God of the eleventh hour. It is never too late for God to show up. He never comes too early or too late; He comes right on time. Don't throw in the towel yet; help is on the way.

Prayer point

Father, make my extremity the beginning of a miracle in Jesus's name.

DAY 41

PERSECUTION

2nd Timothy 3:12, Matthew 5:44

To persecute someone is to treat them cruelly and unfairly, especially because of their race, religion, or political beliefs. Today, we are dealing with the subject of persecution. The Bible says in 2nd Timothy 3:12 that all who will live godly in Christ Jesus shall suffer persecution. We live in a world that hurts God and anything that is associated with Him. People hate God just like they hated Jesus when He was on earth for His earthly ministry. Today, the situation has not gotten any better. The hatred has extended to the Bible and those who believe in God and His word.

In both the old and new testaments, people rose against the only true God. In 1st Peter 4:12-14, the Bible says we should rejoice in the time of persecution. Jesus was ill-treated but took it in good faith. Do not curse, but bless them that accuse you. Pray for those who persecute you. Blessed are those who are persecuted for righteousness for theirs is the kingdom of Heaven (Matthew 5:10-12). Also remember that the sufferings of this world is not as much as the glory that shall be revealed in us in Heaven (Romans 8:18).

Do not think your case is the worst; you need to know what other Christians elsewhere in the world are going through. The Bible even says that a time is coming that those who will kill you will think that they are doing a good deed. Jesus suffered the contradiction of sinners. He endured the suffering so we too should stay loyal to the end to the cause of Christ (Acts 5:40-42).

Prayer point

Father, intervene in nations where Christians are persecuted in Jesus's name.

DAY 42

SERVING GOD

Exodus 23:24-26, Job 36:11, Colossians 3:23-24, Psalm 2:11

God is not looking for workers only, but worshipers. We were created to serve only God and so we are not permitted to serve idols, objects, or other creatures. The Creator is the only one who deserves our service. To serve means to be useful to somebody in achieving or satisfying something. It is to work or perform duties for a person.

According to Exodus 23:24 (NLT), you must not worship the gods of these nations, serve them in any way, or imitate their evil practices. Instead, you must utterly destroy them and smash their sacred pillars. The Bible says in verse 25 of Exodus 23 that, "You must serve only the Lord your God. If you do, I will bless you with food and water, and I will protect you from illness."

You serve God by praying to Him, giving Him thanks, worship, and praise. We serve God by giving Him our time, talents, money, and belongings. We serve God by telling people about His goodness and His loving kindness. We serve

God also by serving our neighbours through giving to our fellow human beings, whether Christian or non-Christian. Service includes giving people our time, advice, and materials, visiting orphans, widows, the homeless, and old people.

There are benefits to serving God through Jesus and in the power of the Holy Spirit. These are:

- He protects us from evil.
- He delivers us.
- He gives us food and water.
- He makes the barren fruitful.
- He daily loads us with benefits.
- He gives us long-time prosperity (Daniel 3:16-18).

Therefore, serve the Lord with trembling and fear, joy, gladness of heart, holiness and a pure heart.

Prayer point

I pull down idols in our land in Jesus's name.

DAY 43

HE THAT WINS SOULS IS WISE

Psalm 126, Matthew 4:19-20, Mark 16:15, Daniel 12:3

"They that turn many to righteousness are as the stars for ever and ever." God is not willing that any should go to hell. There is Heaven to gain when one repents and accepts Jesus as their Lord and Saviour. Rejecting Christ leads to hell. God wants all men to repent; to turn from sin and turn to God and it is our duty as Christians to share the good news (the Gospel).

Acts 10:38 says, "Jesus went about doing good, healing the sick and the oppressed." Let us be wise and preach the gospel, and not share the punishment meant for sinners (1st Corinthians 9:16).

Prayer point

Oh Lord, fill me with the zeal to win souls for Your kingdom.

DAY 44

WHAT TO EXPECT IN TIMES OF REVIVAL

Psalm 85:1-9

Revival is the extraordinary work of God. There is need for more of God in our time. Like Gideon asked in Judges 6: 10-14, "Where are the miracles which our fathers told us about?"

The Bible says in Psalm 85: 1-9:

> *¹ LORD, you poured out blessings on your land!*
> *You restored the fortunes of Israel.*
> *² You forgave the guilt of your people—*
> *yes, you covered all their sins. [Interlude]*
> *³ You held back your fury.*
> *⁴ Now restore us again, O God of our salvation.*
> *Put aside your anger against us once more.*
> *⁵ Will you be angry with us always?*
> *Will you prolong your wrath to all generations?*
> *⁶ Won't you revive us again,*
> *so your people can rejoice in you?*

⁷ Show us your unfailing love, O LORD,
and grant us your salvation.
⁸ I listen carefully to what God the LORD is saying,
for he speaks peace to his faithful people.
But let them not return to their foolish ways.
⁹ Surely his salvation is near to those who fear him,
so our land will be filled with his glory.

The Psalmist observed that God had been favourable unto them as a nation and God will do it again in our time. The issue of forgiveness was raised; the anger of God was turned away. Salvation is the key in the time of revival and this is when the Christian is made to realise the blessings and reality of salvation (2ⁿᵈ Corinthians 5:17).

The big question is will you not revive us so that your people rejoice in you? In times of revival, God speaks peace, with nothing missing. God's expectation is that His people do not return to any foolish acts.

DAY 45

WHAT TO EXPECT IN TIMES OF REVIVAL (PART II)

- ♦ Passion for God.

- ♦ Joy in the Lord.

- ♦ Increase in intercessory prayer.

- ♦ Commitment to fasting.

- ♦ Hunger for the Bible.

- ♦ Increased family spiritual life.

- ♦ General support of God's work.

- ♦ The body of Christ becomes a team.

Prayer point

Lord, I expect repentance, salvation and healing in our revival.

DAY 46

DIVINE GUIDANCE
Psalm 32:8-9, Isaiah 30:21

Life is full of challenges, and decisions must be made for one to know which way to go in life. However, God is ready to guide His children even on a daily basis. It then becomes a matter of choice whether to let God guide us. Psalm 25:14 says that the secret of the Lord is with those who fear Him, and He will show them His covenant.

Psalms 32:8-9 says,

[8] I will instruct you and teach you in the way you should go;
I will guide you with My eye.
[9] Do not be like the horse or like the mule,
Which have no understanding,
Which must be harnessed with bit and bridle,
Else they will not come near you.

We can receive divine direction in the following ways:

- ◆ The word of God (the Bible).
- ◆ Circumstances.

- ♦ Dreams.

- ♦ Visions.

- ♦ Prophecy.

- ♦ Older mature Christians.

- ♦ Sanctified common sense.

The word of God: Is a powerful source of divine direction/guidance. Psalm 119:105 says, "Your word is a lamp to my feet and a light to my path." The devil hinders people from reading the Bible because it enlightens their spiritual eyes to things which ordinary eyes cannot see. Read up Daniel 2:22, Hebrews 4:12 and Romans 8:13-14.

Circumstances: God directs His children even if it doesn't seem like He is involved. He connects you to people and places for reasons best known to Him alone. God brings people into our lives and us into other people's lives at a particular time in life. He also opens doors and closes them through situations.

Dreams: Are visions of the night. They occur when one is asleep. Dreams have played a big role in the Bible and have brought joy and pain to people. Jacob dreamt, Joseph dreamt, Pharaoh dreamt and Nebuchadnezzar dreamt. Joseph dreamt of his destiny, Pharaoh dreamt of the coming bumper harvest and the famine that was to follow, Jesus's earthly parents dreamt of the plot to get rid of Jesus and were warned to take the child and the mother to Egypt. Later on, angels came and told them to take the child back because those who sought the child's life were dead. Lives were spared and disaster was averted (Matthew 2:30).

Prayer point

Lord, give me divine guidance in Jesus's name.

DAY 47

DIVINE GUIDANCE (PART II)

Acts 18:9-10, Acts 27:21-27, Joel 2

Divine guidance: Is the means by which divine messages are communicated. It is divine communication that is seen (Acts 2:17).

Prophecy: Has to do with foretelling what is about to happen, declaring things as inspired by the Holy Spirit through a channel or a prophet who is ordained to speak. It is to speak God's message to the people, to declare His mind to a person or a people. The prophet, who is the mouthpiece of God, takes the problem of the people to God and get messages to the people (Amos 3:7). The purpose of prophets is to edify, establish in faith, comfort and exhort believers. Prophecy might also be to warn people unto repentance. For example, Prophet Agabus in Acts 11: 29 prophesied of famine and Prophet Isaiah spoke of the birth of the Messiah.

Older matured Christians: There's a parable that a young person may have so many new clothes but an older has many old clothes/rags. Youths have strength but elders have grey hairs as their pride. Maturity comes with a wealth of experience. An example was when Jethro saw how Moses, his son in-law, was worn out from judging the people he led, and advised him to choose people to delegate duties to in order to lighten his burden (Exodus 18:17-27).

Sanctified common sense: A man of God once said that God gave you common sense so He can rest. We have the senses of smell, touch, taste, sight and hearing. We must submit these senses to God for Him to sanctify them so we can use them to get messages from Him. The Holy Spirit's fire can sanctify them like in Isaiah's time. God put coal of fire on his tongue to take away his sin (Isaiah 6:7).

Prayer point

Oh Lord, I ask for your divine guidance in every area of my life.

DAY 48

TIME

**Ecclesiastes 3: 1-8, Psalms 102: 12-13,
Ephesians 5:16, 2 Corinthians 6:2, Galatians 4:4**

What is time? It is a measurable period consisting of minutes, days, weeks, months, years, decades and centuries. Time is also defined as an opportunity or season. Ecclesiastes 3:1-4 says,

1 To everything there is a season,
A time for every purpose under Heaven:

2 A time to be born,
And a time to die;
A time to plant,
And a time to pluck what is planted;
3 A time to kill,
And a time to heal;
A time to break down,
And a time to build up;
4 A time to weep,
And a time to laugh;

A time to mourn,
And a time to dance.

Time could be past, present, or futuristic. It is what makes the difference between the rich and the poor. Both classes of people have twenty-four hours at their disposal each day but they spend it differently. The best way to spend time is to invest it. This is what decides the level you get to in life. Do not waste your time instead give it to worthy causes. You are a steward of your time, relationships, money, and talents.

The Bible says that **now** is the time to repent and be saved. It is time to awake from your spiritual sleep, it is time to arise and shine and be counted for God. Pay the tithe of your time. It is time to receive God's mercy and be favoured by God. Now is the time to serve God. Think of the reward that waits for those who labour for things that have eternal value. It is time to think of the judgement day that awaits the people who reject God's mercy.

Prayer point

Oh God, my father, help me to use my time on this earth well.

DAY 49

VISION

Habakkuk 2:2-3, Proverbs 29:18

Myles Munroe of Blessed Memory, in his book, *Principles and Power of Vision*, said, "Physical blindness can do little or no harm, but a man without vision can be limited and may not have appreciable success in life." Lack of wisdom is one of the worst things that can happen to an individual. Proverbs 29:18 says, "Where there is no vision the people perish but he that keeps the law happy is he." In Habakkuk 2:2-3, the Bible enjoins us to write the vision and make it plain.

It makes a whole lot of sense to write down the vision God gave you. Make it easy for others to read. God has destiny helpers strategically positioned to assist you on the way to your destiny. Therefore, write down your vision so that it will not be complicated for your helpers, the people God orchestrated into your life to help interpret your dreams or who come your way to have their dreams interpreted by you.

A vision is for an appointed time. Don't be in a hurry; wait for it. It is only a matter of time. It will surely come to pass. It is a mental picture of where God is taking you in life, or what He wants you to do for Him. A vision is a clear conception of something that is not yet a reality but can exist. Ask God to confirm what He has put in your heart for you to do.

A vision is a strong image of a preferable future and there are principles for fulfilling personal vision.

- ♦ Let your vision be clear.
- ♦ Know your potential to fulfil your vision.
- ♦ Develop a concrete plan for fulfilling your vision.
- ♦ Possess the passion for the vision.
- ♦ Develop faith in the vision.
- ♦ Understand the process for the vision.
- ♦ Set priorities for the vision.
- ♦ Be persistent and patient.
- ♦ Stay connected to the source of your vision

DAY 50

VICTORY

1st John 5:4-5, Revelation 12:11, 1st John 4:4

What is victory?

What are the steps to victory?

What is Christian victory?

We are called to live a life of victory daily.

Fight and you will get victory (Romans 8:31).

David had victory over Goliath (1 Samuel 17).

Fight the good fight of faith, life is a battle and faith is the key to victory.

Prayer point

Oh Lord, may I achieve victory in every area of my life in Jesus's name.

DAY 51

GOD'S FAITHFULNESS

Numbers 23:19, 1st Thessalonians 5:24

God is the supreme creator and owner of Heaven and earth. He is the father of those who believe in his son, Jesus Christ. God is faithful to keep His promises. Faithful is He who called you for He will do what He has promised, and cannot deny Himself.

Be faithful to God in the vows you have made to Him, specifically to serve Him all the days of your life and God will keep His promise. God wants us to be reliable and dependable. He wants husbands and wives to be faithful to each other, and workers to be faithful to their employers.

Prayer point

Oh Lord, you have never failed. Help me to put all my trust in you and in your promises.

DAY 52

SEEK GOD'S KINGDOM FIRST

Matthew 6:33, Micah 6:8, Romans 13:8

"Seek first God's kingdom and its righteousness, and all these things shall be added." Give God's kingdom a priority, put Jesus Christ and the things of God first. We are always tempted to give the things of this world priority. However, God wants us to give things that pertain to the trinity (God the Father, the Son, and the Holy Spirit) first place in our daily choices. Sadly, things that have no Heavenly value call for and grab our attention daily. An average person values issues about food, clothing, and shelter.

We need to preach to those who are not saved, feed the poor, show love to our neighbours, be kind, just, humble, and pray for the needs of our world.

Prayer point

Oh Lord, give me the wisdom to prioritise You and Your kingdom above all else.

DAY 53

GIVE AND IT SHALL BE GIVEN UNTO YOU

Luke 6:38, Psalm 126, Acts 20:35

Most people are good at receiving. Life, however, is not all about receiving. It is about both giving and receiving. A man gives seed to his wife and it becomes a child; a farmer plants seeds in the soil and the seeds germinate and become corn, rice, beans, etc.

If there is no sowing, there will be no harvest. Sowing is not palatable, but reaping is joyful. The Bible says that it is more blessed to give than to receive. We need to be careful what we sow or give. Let the seed you sow be of a high quality.

Prayer point

Oh Lord, give me the spirit of a giver. More so, a cheerful one.

DAY 54

I WILL RESTORE ALL THAT THE ENEMY HAS STOLEN

Jeremiah 30:17, Joel 2:21-25, Psalm 23, Psalm 51:12

God promised to restore all that the enemy, the devil, has stolen. That means He will bring back from captivity, or return something to its former owner, in the same condition or position it was found.

God promises to restore health to those who are sick or carried to captivity. Also, God will restore the years the locust has eaten.

Prayer point

May God's restoration affect my life and the church as a collective in Jesus's name.

DAY 55

VESSEL UNTO HONOUR

2nd Timothy 2:20, 1st Kings 4:1-7

A vessel is used to hold liquid or other substances. In the Holy Scriptures, vessels are sometimes used to refer to human beings. Any person God has called, He uses.

There are both vessels unto honour, and vessels unto dishonour. Vessels unto honour are those that are displayed in public, while vessels unto dishonour are not proudly displayed. As a child of God, you should strive to be a vessel unto honour.

Prayer point

Oh Lord, my father, may I be a vessel unto honour, fit for Your use.

DAY 56

CASTING OUT DEMONS
Matthew 12:27-28, Luke 10:19-20, Mark 14:17

There are demons all over the world. The Bible recognises angels and demons in both the old and new testaments. The Bible commands us to rebuke and cast out evil spirits. It is not for show.

Those possessed or oppressed by demons are not to be entertained or used for entertainment. The person must repent and present themselves to have the demons within cast out so they can make room for Jesus to live within them.

Prayer point

I command any demon within me to leave permanently in Jesus's name.

98

DAY 57

A GODLY LEADER

Matthew 20:26, 1ˢᵗ Timothy 3:1-4

There are various types of leaders. You can be the leader of a family (father or mother), the leader of a political group, or the leader of a cultural group. The work of a godly leader is to hear from God and relay whatever message is received from God to the followers. The world is currently in short supply of godly leaders. We need more leaders who are prayerful.

According to John Maxwell, a good leader should have integrity, show good examples, be hardworking, God-fearing, and have the ability to direct and communicate. Examples of leaders in the Bible include, but are not limited to, Abraham, Moses, David, Joshua, and Paul.

A good leader possesses the following qualities:

- ♦ Modesty.
- ♦ Honesty.
- ♦ Integrity.
- ♦ Humility.

Prayer point

Oh Lord, make me a godly leader in this generation for Your glory and to the benefit of mankind.

DAY 58

⚜

THE CHRISTIAN HOME
Psalm 127, Psalm 128

The Christian home has been a centre for contention since the beginning of time up until now. The devil often directs his aggression at whatever God is interested in.

The devil fought the first family (Adam and Eve's family). He brought temptation, deception, and tried to counterfeit God's word, which caused distractions and animosity within that family just to derail them from God's plans and intentions for them.

There are various keys to success within the home. Some of these keys are:

- ♦ Love and unity between parents.
- ♦ Godly children.
- ♦ Security.
- ♦ Teamwork and collaboration between family members.

A family that prays together, stays together. For a family to thrive, all family members must have the fear of God (Psalm 128, Ephesians 6:11-14). Let Jesus be the head of your home.

Prayer point

Lord, let my home reflect your glory.

DAY 59

ELIJAH, A PROPHET OF GOD

1ˢᵗ Kings 18:1-46, James 5:17-18

Elijah is one of the well-known prophets of God in the Bible. He performed various exploits using the power of God. He challenged the prophets of Baal to a contest to know which of the two parties served the living God. During his confrontation with those false prophets, Elijah declared the following, "The God that answers by fire, let him be God."

Another of Elijah's notable exploits was praying and shutting the windows of Heaven so that there would be no rain for three and a half years, and then praying again so that the Heavens would open again and release rain.

Elijah parted River Jordan and defended the name of Yahweh. He was taken to Heaven on a chariot of fire, and did not taste death like Enoch. He was a man of faith and we should follow in his footsteps and walk by faith as well.

Prayer point

Oh Lord, God of Elijah, grant me the faith and power to perform exploits and defend Your name like Elijah did.

DAY 60

THE NAMES OF GOD
Proverbs 18:10, Matthew 1:21

A name provides identity. The names people bear are often influenced by the circumstances surrounding their births. Names in various cultures have a plethora of hidden, deeper meanings. In the Hebrew culture, names are very significant.

Our God has many names, some of which are.

- ◆ Jehovah Jireh – The Lord our provider (Genesis 22:14)
- ◆ Jehovah Shalom – God, our peace (Judges 6:24)
- ◆ Jehovah Nissi – The Lord our banner (Exodus 17:15)
- ◆ Jehovah Rohi – God, our Shepherd (Psalm 23:1)
- ◆ Jehovah Rapha – The Lord, our Healer (Exodus 15:26)

Call upon the names of the Lord and you shall be saved.

Prayer point

Oh Lord, give me the wisdom to call upon your name in the time of trouble.

ABOUT THE AUTHOR

Pastor Peter Friday Ajayi joined full-time ministry in The Apostolic Church in 1991. In 1997, he graduated from The Apostolic Church Theological Seminary, Ilesha, Osun State, Nigeria. Following his relocation to South Africa, he obtained B.Th. from the Baptist Theological College, Randburg, South Africa in 2008. He is married to Deaconess Grace Iyabo Ajayi, and they are blessed with children.

He is a popular conference speaker, TV guest and marriage counsellor.

www.ingramcontent.com/pod-product-compliance
Lightning Source LLC
LaVergne TN
LVHW041302080426
835510LV00009B/837